FaithMoves
in Forty Days Closer to Him

———◇◆◇———

Teri Gallo Blackadar

ISBN 978-1-0980-9258-0 (paperback)
ISBN 978-1-0980-9260-3 (hardcover)
ISBN 978-1-0980-9259-7 (digital)

Christian Faith Publishing, Inc.
832 Park Avenue
Meadville, PA 16335
www.christianfaithpublishing.com

ALL Bible texts are from The Jentezen Franklin Legacy Study Bible NKJV Copoyright 2018 by Jentezen Franklin

EXCEPT the Bible verse in the Preface is taken from: The Everyday Life Bible (Amplified Bible) October 2014

Printed in the United States of America

In the memory of Duna Blackadar, who believed I am a writer.
To Louis Gallo, who taught me faith.

For assuredly I say to you, if you have faith as
a mustard seed, you will say to this mountain,
"Move from here to there," and it will move;
and nothing will be impossible for you.
—Matthew 17:20 (NKJV)

CONTENTS

INTRODUCTION

Several years ago, while living through a valley of loss, grief, and an incredible amount of change, the Lord gave me enormous strength and revealed to me that I would have to trust Him and allow Him to carry me "from here to there," much as the mountain parable in Matthew 17:20.

FaithMoves was initially the name I coined for a fitness stretching class that I taught, which moved the body and spine accompanied by popular Christian melodies. I included a topic with each class and choreographed music on a playlist to complement it. The seed for a devotional style book was planted.

I came to realize over the years since then just how much *FaithMoves* in my life and in your life also! James wrote, "So too, faith, if it does not have works (to back it up), is by itself dead (inoperative and ineffective)" (James 2:17 AMP). I believe that when we intentionally move our faith, it is only then that we can bear good fruit.

I believe that I must move spiritually each day in various ways to activate faith. With this I am able to transform and create as He wills. I can hear God's voice, then act on it. Move means to act. Faith is an act—an act with intention. *FaithMoves* in relationship with Jesus. *FaithMoves* in praise, worship, gratitude, surrender, generosity, brokenness, and love…and so much more! Thank you, Lord, for the precious gift of faith.

How to get optimal use of this book for a deeper study to activate your faith? It is written in simple format to allow for a forty-day journey and/or daily devotion on various topics and circumstances that are relevant for you.

1. Read the scriptures beneath the topic and spend some time in silence asking God to reveal His truth to you, then read the reflection on the topic.
2. Commence to pray the personal prayer.
3. Speak the scripture verses out loud.

Confessing and declaring God's Word out loud vibrates His promises and is a powerful act of faith.

> For as the rain comes down and the snow from heaven and do not return there but water the earth and make it bring forth and bud that it may give seed to the sower and bread to the eater, so shall My Words be that goes forth from My mouth; it shall not return to Me void, but it shall accomplish what I please, and it shall prosper in the thing for which I sent it. (Isaiah. 55:10–11 NKJV)

1

FaithMoves in Pursuit of Holiness

> Blessed are the pure in heart, for they shall see God. (Matthew 5:8 NKJV)

> He chose us in Him before the foundation of the world that we should be holy and without blame before Him in love. (Ephesians 1:4 NKJV)

Our faith is holy and pleasing to God. *FaithMoves* toward Him in abundant passion. To choose holiness can mean turning away from anything which is not or to refrain from speaking the first thing that comes to mind. The Holy Spirit corrects us when our thoughts are not of God. Paul instructed Timothy, "But in a great house, there are not only vessels of gold and silver but also of wood and clay, some for honor and some for dishonor. Therefore, if anyone cleanses himself from the latter, he will be a vessel of honor, sanctified and useful for the Master, prepared for every good work" (2 Timothy 2:20–21 NKJV).

Is this a lofty or unattainable ideal? Holiness begins in the mind and heart. Our thoughts become our words and actions. "For as he thinks in his heart, so is he" (Proverbs 23:7 NKJV). In our human-ness, we are weak, yet God knows everything concerning us. During these times, He will lift us up, and we will once again set our intentions on pleasing Him. Our spirits are to be aligned with His Spirit. That is His will for us. We pray for realignment. Faith will prevail when pride is snuffed out.

To pursue our Lord with fervor and tenacity is a daily choice. Holiness and purity depend on abiding in Him. So when the Holy Spirit nudges us with conviction, we are able to hear. It is always a decision to live the way He desires us to live. This choice sets us apart before Him. It is His will for us. "Be holy, for I am holy" (1 Peter 1:16 NKJV).

Pray

Dear Lord, I want my faith to sustain me as you refine me like silver and gold. Please change my heart and guard my mouth each day. When I fail, please pick me up quickly, and I will repent. And purify my thoughts, Lord. Burn away all those that tarnish holiness. In Jesus's name.

Confess

> Create in me a clean heart, O God, and renew a steadfast spirit within me. Do not cast me away from Your presence, and do not take Your Holy Spirit from me. (Psalm 51:10–11 NKJV)

> Let the words of my mouth and the meditation of my heart be acceptable in Your sight, O Lord, my strength and my redeemer. (Psalm 19:14 NKJV)

2

FaithMoves Forward

Reflect

> Whenever the cloud was taken up from above the tabernacle after that the children of Israel would journey and in the place where the cloud settled, there the children of Israel would pitch their tents. (Numbers 9:17 NKJV)

> Behold, I will do a new thing, now it shall spring forth; shall you not know it? I will even make a road in the wilderness and rivers in the desert. (Isaiah 43:19 NKJV)

The children of Israel moved camp when the cloud moved. Often we find ourselves looking for a sign that God undoubtedly wants us to go forward in a given situation or just camp where we are. *FaithMoves* when we take small steps in the direction He is leading. Stubbornly, we may dig our heels in and not budge. Of course, He allows such free will on our part, yet that usually is not His best for us.

Moving forward can create anxiety, fear, indecision, and a good case of the what-ifs within us. When this happens—and it is likely to—you become Satan's target when you are moving forward in God's plan and purpose for your life. Remember God's promise: "Be strong and of good courage, do not fear nor be afraid of them; for the Lord God, He is the One who goes with you. He will not leave you nor forsake you" (Deuteronomy 31:21 NKJV).

FaithMoves forward in a continuum. Each step is an act of obedience. Allow Him to direct your steps this day. Walk along the path He designed just for you. The path is His Word. While He was standing on the water, Jesus told Peter to "come" to Him. Walk on His Word, not the water. It was never about the water.

Pray

Dear Lord, I want to walk in faith. I cannot see beyond today, but You can. Help me to trust You in each step taken that I believe the direction is Your will for my life. I surrender each step to You, knowing Your grace will be sufficient as my faith deepens as I step forward. In Jesus's name.

Confess

I cast all my cares upon Him, for He cares for me. (1 Peter 5:7 NKJV)

Teach me Your way, O Lord, and lead me in a smooth path. (Psalm 27:11 NKJV)

3

FaithMoves in Awe of His Power

Reflect

> In the beginning God created the heavens and the earth. Then God saw everything He had made, and indeed it was very good. (Genesis 1:1,31 NKJV)

> For God so loved the world that He gave His only begotten Son that whoever believes in Him should not perish but have everlasting life. (John 3:16 NKJV)

Such love as this! In the cyclic movement of our earth and its seasons, we receive nourishment when the Son, light of His Spirit, feeds our hearts. Regardless of where you are, look and see the artwork of our Creator in the diverse landscapes of our world even in cities where architectural beauty can envelope the surroundings. God gave all men creative abilities. Such is the wonder of our minds! How He loves us!

When we pay attention, we see we are surrounded by His magnificence. Often we can take for granted the intricacies of the human body along with every bird, animal, fish, insect, rock, seashell, plant, herb, tree, fruit, and vegetable that He made for a purpose. Such an imagination He possesses! The sea, mountains, sun, moon, and stars shout of His majesty. *FaithMoves* in awe of it all.

Paul prayed that "Christ may dwell in your hearts through faith; that you, being rooted and grounded in love, may be able to comprehend with all the saints what is the width and length and depth and height—to know the love of Christ which passes knowledge; that you may be filled with all the fullness of God" (Ephesians 3:17–19 NKJV). This indeed is a powerful prayer and one to declare for ourselves and those we love. Be in awe today of God's power and love for us. There is nothing impossible for Him.

Pray

Dear Lord, I thank you this day that I am created by You for a specific purpose. You loved the world so much that you sent Jesus to die for me so that I may be filled with Your spirit. In Your power, Jesus was raised from the dead to sit next to You in heaven. Please continue to reveal Your power in my life that I may be in Your will each day and use the gifts you have given me. In Jesus name.

Confess

I know that whatever God does, it shall be forever. Nothing can be added to it, and nothing can be taken from it. God does it that men should fear before Him. (Ecclesiastes 3:14 NKJV)

My faith does not rest in the wisdom of men but in the power of God. (1 Corinthians 2:5 NKJV)

4

FaithMoves in Silence

Reflect

> Be still, and know that I am God; I will be exalted among the nations, I will be exalted in the earth! (Psalm 46:10 NKJV)

> My voice You shall hear in the morning, O Lord; in the morning, I will direct it to You, and I will look up. (Psalm 5:3 NKJV)

Notwithstanding every single device, media, apps, work, family, obligations, and distractions in our daily lives, God seeks us to be still. How else can we ever hear His voice, His guidance? Satan knows this all too well. We may be born again, believers in Jesus, yet unable to deepen our faith and relationship with Him until we commit time, preferably the first part of our day, to be in communication with Him.

Satan is a thief and will try to steal this time from us anyway he can—the phone, the baby crying, oversleeping, social media, almost anything that keeps us from drawing close to God. We reassure ourselves as we're running out the door that we will get in His Word later. Satan is also the father of all lies. *FaithMoves* when you stand strong in stillness, and your eyes are fixed on Him.

During our morning prayer, we have His attention because we are putting Him first. He will bless this faithfulness on our part. In the pauses between our prayers, the Holy Spirit will bring fresh revelations to our minds, necessary convictions, the guidance we need, and discernment for whatever comes up throughout the day. We will recognize His still small voice in the silence. "Your ears shall hear a word behind you, saying, 'This is the way, walk in it'" (Isaiah 30:21 NKJV). That is His promise.

Pray

Dear Lord, I believe *FaithMoves* in silence. Allow me to be still long enough to hear Your voice. Help me to put away any distractions that keep us apart. Help me to discern between the mind chatter of my own voice, Your voice, and that of the enemy. Whatever You are trying to say to me, I am listening. I want a deeper relationship with you, Lord. Let it begin today. In Jesus's name.

Confess

Today I will hear His voice and harden not my heart. (Psalm 95: 7b, 8 NKJV)

I am one of Your sheep, Lord, and I will hear Your voice and follow You. (John 10:27 NKJV)

5

FaithMoves in Thanksgiving

Reflect

> In everything, give thanks; for this is the will
> of God in Christ Jesus for you. (1 Thessalonians
> 5:18 NKJV)

> I will praise You, for I am fearfully and
> wonderfully made, marvelous are Your works,
> and that my soul knows very well. (Psalm 139:14
> NKJV)

So often we struggle with knowing God's will for our lives. In these moments, it is helpful to get back to basics. Let's begin with thanking Him. Our very beings exist in His world for a purpose. We are made in His image yet distinct like no other. He pours blessings and spiritual gifts on us. "Know that the Lord, He is God. It is He who has made us and not we ourselves; we are His people and the sheep of His pasture" (Psalm 100:3 NKJV).

Comparing ourselves with others breaks His heart. Grumbling and complaining quench the Holy Spirit. In our humanness (and with Satan's help), we allow our minds to drift away in discouragement, envy, selfishness, and pride. Fortunately, His strength is made perfect in our weakness (2 Corinthians 12:9). When we call out to

Him with thanksgiving and praise, He hears us. *FaithMoves* us into a new perspective. We are able to see the blessings all around us—specific treasures that are uniquely ours.

God's Word is God's will. It is His will for us to have hearts of gratitude despite our feelings or circumstances. Job is the perfect example of a man who lost so much and suffered hardships, yet his faith gave him strength. "Shall we indeed accept good from God, and shall we not accept adversity" (Job 2:10 NKJV)? God will always honor our praise and thanksgiving during times of pain and brokenness.

Pray

Dear Lord, thank You for this day, for my breath, and my life. I know that every good and perfect gift comes from You. Thank You, Holy Spirit, for Your anointing. I offer my life back to You as a living sacrifice. I need Your help in my weaknesses. Give me the courage and strength to be an overcomer. Let holiness be an offering of gratitude to You. In Jesus's name.

Confess

I will enter Your gate with thanksgiving and into Your court with praise. I am thankful to you and bless Your name. (Psalm 100:4 NKJV)

The Lord is good; for His mercy, tender kindness, and steadfast love endure forever." (Jeremiah 33:11 NKJV)

6

FaithMoves with His Grace

Reflect

> For by grace, you have been saved through faith and that not of yourselves; it is the gift of God. (Ephesians 2:8 NKJV)

> For all have sinned and fall short of the glory of God, being justified freely by His grace through the redemption that is in Christ Jesus. (Romans 3:23–24 NKJV)

It was our faith that opened our hearts into a relationship with Jesus. It is God's grace which prepares the way back to Him when we wander too far. It is His unmerited favor, always present in our lives, that woos us into His fold again.

God's Word says that where sin abounds, grace abounds much more (Romans 5:20). Yes, grace does cover a multitude of sins, and we do have a sin nature, yet because *FaithMoves* in our lives, we don't want to continue living that way. We truly desire to be holy and pleasing to Him who gives us so much grace. The Holy Spirit is right there inside of us to convict us of truth and help us to change. We only need to receive it.

Abraham and his wife, Sarah, had strong faith and were obedient to God's calling to leave their country. They even had a bit of faith when God promised them a family, yet they took matters into their own hands. We are no different. How often do we take our will back? How often does our faith waver? *Did God really say...?* It is during those times that He pours out more grace over our circumstances. He loves us anyway.

Pray

Dear Lord, thank You for Your amazing grace each day. Even when I let you down over and over again, Your grace surrounds me. Help me to get up when I fall and once again to seek You with all my heart, soul, mind, and strength. Thank You for Your gift of grace. In Jesus's name.

Confess

> I am growing and becoming strong in spirit, filled with wisdom; and the grace of God is upon me. (Luke 2:40 NKJV)

> His grace is sufficient for me; for His power is being perfected in my weakness. (2 Corinthians 12:9 NKJV)

7

FaithMoves in Forgiveness

Reflect

> And whenever you stand praying, if you have anything against anyone, forgive him, that your Father in heaven may also forgive you your trespasses. But if you do not forgive, neither will your Father in heaven forgive your trespasses. (Mark 11:25–26 NKJV)

> I acknowledged my sin to You, and my iniquity I have not hidden. I said, "I will confess my transgressions to the Lord," and You forgave the iniquity of my sin. (Psalm 32:5 NKJV)

Adam and Eve attempted to hide from God in the garden after they were deceived by Satan. God knew what occurred, yet He asked them, "Who told you were naked? Have you eaten from the tree of which I commanded you that you should not eat" (Genesis 3:12 NKJV)? At first, Adam rationalized the situation and blamed Eve. Then they confessed to God what had occurred. This was the first confession, and even though God was angry, and there were consequences, He forgave them.

Throughout Bible history, God's people have let Him down repeatedly. We also sin and fail God and ourselves over and over again. *FaithMoves* in repentance and forgiveness. Jesus died for us—the ultimate sacrifice and act of God's unconditional love for His people. Know the power of His forgiveness. The Holy Spirit will give us the same power to forgive others who hurt us and let us down.

The enemy relentlessly attempts to remind us of our past. It can be pure torture if we fail to take these thoughts captive. God loves us. Jesus died for our sins. We are cleansed by His blood and have a renewed mind and nature. To forgive others and ourselves is a powerful act of faith which moves us to a place of emotional healing.

Pray

Dear Lord, I am sorry for all the ways I have let you down by my thoughts and deeds; by selfishness, self-pity, and dishonesty (be specific here). Please forgive me, and I will also forgive others that have hurt me (specific names). Bless them as I would want to be blessed. Help me, Lord, when the enemy tells me I am not worthy so that I can forgive myself. In Jesus's name.

Confess

I am kind to one another, tenderhearted, forgiving one another, even as God in Christ forgave me. (Ephesians 4:32 NKJV)

I will forgive up to seventy times seven times. (Matthew 22:18 NKJV)

8

FaithMoves in Wisdom

Reflect

> If any of you lacks wisdom, let him ask of God who gives to all liberally and without reproach, and it will be given to him. But let him ask in faith with no doubting, for he who doubts is like a wave of the sea driven and tossed by the wind. (James 1:5–6 NKJV)

> For the Lord gives wisdom; from His mouth comes knowledge and understanding. (Proverbs 2:6 NKJV)

Such a wonderful promise our Lord gives us! He will provide an overabundance of wisdom by simply asking in faith. In Proverbs 4:6–7 (NKJV), wisdom is exalted! "Do not forsake her, and she will preserve you; love her, and she will keep you. Wisdom is the principal thing; therefore, get wisdom." God's Word is not only His will for us, it is also His wisdom. *FaithMoves* in truth and discernment, which only the Holy Spirit can stir within.

How much of our lives have been a cleanup of poor judgments and wrong choices? How often do we want what we want and neglect going to Him first and asking for His divine wisdom? Fortunately for us, He teaches us through our errors and makes something good come from our messes.

Our decisions define us; they can create joy or pain in our life. *FaithMoves* in wisdom in order to know His purpose. It brings the right people to consult, the right place and time to establish His plan. Often the hard decisions are the correct choices. Pray and pause and listen. We can be certain that when we walk in wisdom, God is walking along side us.

———◇✦◇———

Pray

Dear Lord, today when I seek Your presence, I ask for wisdom in all areas of my life (include any specific area). Thank You for providing the answers and direction I need to be in alignment with Your purpose for my life. Strengthen my faith so that I will not doubt the still small voice of Your Spirit. In Jesus's name.

Confess

Wisdom is better than rubies, and all the things one may desire cannot be compared to her. (Proverbs 8:11 NKJV)

I am confident of this very thing, that He who has begun a good work in me will complete it until the day of Jesus Christ. (Philippians 1:6 NKJV)

9

FaithMoves with Spiritual Gifts

Reflect

> There are diversities of gifts but the same Spirit. There are differences of ministries but the same Lord. And there are diversities of activities, but it is the same God who works all in all. But the manifestation of the Spirit is given to each one for the profit of all. (1 Corinthians 12:4–7NKJV)

> For to one is given the word of wisdom through the Spirit, to another the word of knowledge through the same Spirit, to another faith by the same Spirit, to another gifts of healing by the same Spirit, to another the working of miracles, to another prophesy, to another discerning of spirits, to another different kinds of tongues, to another the interpretation of tongues. (1 Corinthians 12:8–10 NKJV)

There is much to meditate on in these passages. Although a deeper study of spiritual gifts is vital for understanding. *FaithMoves* when we ask God for wisdom and application for ourselves. Further along in

First Corinthians, Paul reveals additional gifts of faith, hope, and love with love being the greatest.

Perhaps you already know the gifts the Holy Spirit has given to you. Some denominations do not emphasize this topic, believing these are only for pastors, ministers, and priests. God's Word clearly states they are for all of us who repent, believe, and have been baptized in Jesus Christ as their Lord and Savior (Acts 2:38–39).

FaithMoves when we ask God to reveal to us our spiritual gifts and then activate them for His glory. The fulfillment of our destiny is in direct proportion to our faith of these gifts. "I have fought the good fight, I have finished the race, I have kept the faith" (2 Timothy 4:7 NKJV). His Word says to earnestly desire these gifts, especially love. Receive them.

Pray

Dear Lord, as I humble myself before You, I ask that You show me the spiritual gifts you gave me and strengthen my faith to use them as You intend me to. I thank You as I know that every good and perfect gift comes from above. You are my Father and want to give wonderful gifts and blessings to all your children, including me. In Jesus's name.

Confess

I have received God's power and spiritual gifts as the Holy Spirit has come upon me. (Acts 1:8 NKJV)

God has anointed me and sealed me and has given me the Spirit in my heart as a guarantee. (2 Corinthians 1:21 NKJV)

10

FaithMoves in Truth

Reflect

In the beginning was the Word, and the Word was with God, and the Word was God. He was in the beginning with God. All things were made through Him, and without Him, nothing was made that was made. In Him was life, and the life was the light of men. And the light shines in the darkness, and the darkness did not comprehend it. (John 1:1–5 NKJV)

The secret of the Lord is with those who fear Him, and He will show them His covenant. (Psalm 25:14 NKJV)

Numerous passages in the Word begin with Jesus saying: "Verily, Verily," "Assuredly I tell you," and "It is written." Jesus spoke truth always. He is the Spirit of truth and the greatest teacher the world has ever known. Every word Jesus spoke to His disciples and followers was truth. He was a teacher of love, wisdom, and forgiveness. His presence was both commanding and compassionate.

FaithMoves when God's Word sinks deep inside the inner man. "Ask and you shall receive. Seek and you will find. Knock and the door will be open" (Matthew 7:7–8). He will not withhold His truth from us, nor His grace, nor His wisdom.

Jesus revealed God's truth and mysteries in multitudes of parables. These teachings have fed His people for centuries through anointed pastors, ministers, and priests. There is no end to the eloquence of His Word and the revelations vital for transformation. His promise is that truth brings freedom. "If you abide in My Word, you are My disciples indeed. And you shall know the truth, and the truth shall make you free" (John 8:31–32 NKJV).

Pray

Dear Lord, thank You for Your Word, Your truth. Please give me a mind and heart that remain open and willing to see, hear, and know that You are God. I will trust and rely on You always. Your truth will be a light unto my path. In Jesus's name.

Confess

I will seek You and find You because I search for You with my whole heart. (Jeremiah 29:13 NKJV)

I have an anointing from the Holy One, and I know all things. (1 John 2:20 NKJV)

11

FaithMoves in Victory

Reflect

> Yours, O Lord, is the greatest, the power and the glory, the victory and the majesty, (1 Chronicles 29:11 NKJV)

> Walk in the Spirit, and you shall not fulfill the lust of the flesh. For the flesh lusts against the Spirit, and the Spirit against the flesh; these are contrary to one another so that you do not do the things you wish. (Galatians 5:16–17 NKJV)

Attempts to defeat works of the flesh (adultery, fornication, uncleanness, lewdness, idolatry, sorcery, hatred, contentions, jealousies, outbursts of wrath, selfish ambitions, dissensions, heresies, envy, murders, drunkenness, revelries, and the like) on self-will will leave us discouraged and ashamed. Only when we repent and surrender, we are restored by His power. The Holy Spirit is our true source to help us be victorious in all circumstances by His gentle convictions.

How often do we begin the day in prayer and resolve that we will not fall into our addictions, wrong attitudes, judgments, and other unbecoming attributes, yet halfway through or by the end of the day there we are, right where we don't want to be. Living a victorious life is not for the fainthearted. "For a righteous man may fall seven times and rise again" (Proverbs 24:16 NKJV). We cannot give up; we must stand up.

FaithMoves when we set our minds on the fruit of the Spirit (love, joy, peace, long-suffering, kindness, goodness, faithfulness, gentleness, and self-control). This is evident when Jesus told Peter to "watch and pray in the garden of Gethsemane instead of sleeping, lest he enters into temptation. Pray in the Spirit. Pray without ceasing. Speak the Word out loud. His victorious power pours out for you.

Pray

Dear Lord, I believe I can fight each battle that comes my way with the Holy Spirit's help and that no weapon formed against me will prosper. I have the mind of Your Son, Jesus, because I believe in Him with all my heart and soul. You are on my side. Please pull down every stronghold that holds me back from living victoriously. In Jesus's name.

Confess

I am more than a conqueror in Him who loves me. (Romans 8:37 NKJV)

I will resist the devil, and he will flee from me. I will draw near to God, and He will draw near to me. (James 4:7–8 NKJV)

12

FaithMoves in Sincerity

Reflect

> You ask and do not receive, because you ask amiss that you may spend it on your pleasures. (James 4:3 NKJV)

> Now therefore, fear the Lord, serve Him in sincerity and in truth, and put away the gods which your fathers served on the other side of the river and in Egypt. Serve the Lord. (Joshua 24:14 NKJV)

There are times even the best of us will serve, give, or act in order to obtain approval of others. Sometimes this is conscious on our part, other times, just old behavior. God's grace will work for us by the Holy Spirit's conviction. Sincerity and right motives are a heart condition. Since God always knows our heart and true motivation, we cannot hide it.

FaithMoves in a mindset that truly wants to please Him with all sincerity. It becomes our nature as we develop a deeper relationship with Him. He wants us to be of service to others yet not so that we are noticed by our works. "But when you do a charitable deed, do not let your left hand know what your right hand is doing, that your

46

charitable deed may be in secret" (Matthew 6:3–4 NKJV). Later in Matthew 6:17, it speaks of fasting in secret as not to be noticed except by God. We fast and pray to draw closer to Him and not to show ourselves devout.

It becomes a spiritually mature and healthy habit to check in with ourselves and inquire, "what is my motivation in this situation?" If it is self-seeking, the Holy Spirit will let you know. In John 12:43 (NKJV), Jesus calls out the Pharisees as loving the praise of men more than the praise of God. People-pleasing may be a stronghold for us, but nothing is too difficult for Him to deliver us from.

Pray

Dear Lord, forgive me for all the times I want approval from others more than You. I want my heart to be sincere in all matters. Holy Spirit, please change my heart. Help me see my motivation before I say or do anything for selfish or self-seeking reasons. Convict me each time I fall into people pleasing behavior. In Jesus's name.

Confess

I live in all good conscience before God. (Acts 23:1 NKJV)

As in water face reflects face, so a man's heart reveals the man. (Proverbs 27:19 NKJV)

13

FaithMoves while Waiting

Reflect

> Therefore, the Lord will wait that He may be gracious to you; and therefore, He will be exalted that He may have mercy on you. For the Lord is a God of justice; blessed are all those who wait for Him. (Isaiah 30:18 NKJV)

> Wait on the Lord; be of good courage, and He shall strengthen your heart; wait, I say on the Lord! (Psalm 27:14 NKJV)

Few things are harder in life than having to wait and to remain patient without complaining. It's easy to give lip service to God's timing, yet it can be difficult to keep the right attitude. Often when we are seeking answers, direction, or have been in the valley of despair for a while, it seems justified to feel frustrated. *When God, when? How God, how?* Our impatience overflows to other areas in our daily life.

His Word says that those that wait for Him will be blessed! During these extended periods, *FaithMoves* us forward. We continue to live for Him through prayer, thanksgiving, praise, worship, and service to others. The answers will come. His promises are for us.

In Isaiah 40:31 (NKJV), it says, "Those who wait on the Lord shall renew their strength."

God's timing is perfect even when it doesn't feel that way. Many a preacher has shared: "God is never early, and He's never late." Best not to take matters in our own hands and kick down unopened doors or use manipulation to obtain things we want. *FaithMoves* with patiently waiting. It is an act of trust and reliance on Him. The interesting paradox is that God waits for us too!

Pray

Dear Lord, I'm sorry for all the times I've tried to make things happen in my own will instead of trusting You. Help me to stand firm in truth and patience. Forgive me of any and all grumbling I have done. Allow my faith to endure and move forward in Your will while I wait for You. Thank You for being patient with me too. In Jesus's name.

Confess

I trust in You, O Lord; You are my God. My times are in Your hand. (Psalm 31:14–15 NKJV)

He has made everything beautiful in its time. (Ecclesiastes 3:11 NKJV)

14

FaithMoves in Generosity

Reflect

> There is one who scatters yet increases more; and there is one who withholds more than is right, but it leads to poverty. The generous soul will be made rich, and he who waters will also be watered himself. (Proverbs 11:24–25 NKJV)

> And I will rebuke the devourer for your sakes so that he will not destroy the fruit of your ground, nor shall the vine fail to bear fruit for you in the field. (Malachi 4:1 NKJV)

Consider the reasons we first give to God. Consider the reasons we give to others and charities throughout the year. Our motivation is paramount. Generosity is an act of faith and obedience not in a self-serving way in order to benefit. Although God promises us that we will be blessed, Jesus also said it is better to give than receive.

FaithMoves with generosity in reflection of our new nature. We belong to His family. When we give first, there is always enough to get by on until our next paycheck. He promises to rebuke the devourer for us. Perhaps we do not experience unexpected expenses as often. Life runs more smoothly financially as *FaithMoves* in generosity. It may do you well to notice the little ways you are blessed that save your resources.

It is amazing how God does math—the resulting way it always works out. There is always enough. Sometimes during financial struggle, it is tempting to want to hold back on giving, yet God truly honors your heart when you give in lack. In Luke 21:1–4 (NKJV), Jesus tells us of the widow who gave two mites for that is all she had. Her faith touched God more than the rich who gave from their abundance.

Pray

Dear Lord, Thank You for all the blessings in my life. Please prepare my heart whenever I give so that it is always with the right motives. Help me to trust you with all my time and resources. I believe Your promises, I believe You will rebuke the devourer on my behalf. I believe You will prosper me and bless me in all I do. In Jesus's name.

Confess

I will prosper in all things and be in health just as my soul prospers. (3 John 2 NKJV)

My prayers and my alms have come up for a memorial before God. (Acts 10:5 NKJV)

15

FaithMoves in Spiritual Warfare

Reflect

> The Lord will cause your enemies who rise against you to be defeated before your face; they shall come out against you one way and flee before you seven ways. (Deuteronomy 28:7 NKJV)

> For we do not wrestle against flesh and blood but against principalities, against powers, against the rulers of the darkness of this age, against spirituals hosts of wickedness in the heavenly places, therefore, take up the whole armor of God. (Ephesians 6:13–14 NKJV)

God promises us that if we obey His voice (Deuteronomy 28:1–2) we will receive blessings, including His protection. Paul also emphasizes in Ephesians 6:14 that if we take up the whole armor of God, we will be able to withstand evil. Noteworthy is that there are seven pieces of armor, and God said our enemies will flee in seven ways.

FaithMoves when we begin each day wearing the full armor of God. His truth around our waist, His righteousness across our chests, the shoes of peace to share His love, the shield of faith in one hand to overcome fear and doubt, while in our other hand, the sword of the Spirit, which is His Word. We put on the helmet of salvation to remember our identity in Him whenever our minds are attacked by the accuser. Lastly, the seventh piece of armor is prayer. Paul instructs us to open our mouths boldly in prayer and supplication in the Spirit.

God's power is ours in every situation and circumstance that is in opposition to His best for our lives. *FaithMoves* for us and in us so that we will stand in victory. We can overcome by His strength as He will fight our battles if we seek Him first.

Pray

Dear Lord, thank You for always being with me in each difficulty and trial I face. Thank You for cleansing my mind from thoughts that are not Yours when I take them captive in obedience. Thank You, Holy Spirit, for discernment to know Satan's plots against me and for the courage to resist him. In Jesus's name.

Confess

I am more than a conqueror through Him who loves me. (Romans 8:37 NKJV)

God has not given me a spirit of fear but of power and love and a sound mind. (1 Timothy 1:7 NKJV)

16

FaithMoves Resting in His Presence

Reflect

> Then the apostles gathered to Jesus and told Him all things, both what they had done and what they had taught. And He said to them, "Come aside by yourselves to a deserted place and rest a while." (Mark 6:30–31 NKJV)

> Come to Me, all you who labor and are heavy laden, and I will give you rest. Take My yoke upon you and learn from Me, for I am gentle and lowly in heart, and you will find rest for your souls. (Matthew 11:28–29 NKJV)

These twenty-first century times, although He handpicked for us to be alive now, are in perpetual motion with every increasing stimulation to all of our senses. Some days it is just too much. Our brains are His handiwork of nerve circuitry, yet too often, we find ourselves overwhelmed by the sheer amount of knowledge, details, and data bombarding us. How can we even think, let alone hear His voice in all the static!

When we deliberately pause, reset, turn off, and go within, *FaithMoves* us closer to Him. Jeremiah 29:13 (NKJV) emphatically promises us that if we seek Him, we will find Him when we search for Him with our whole heart. He promises to bring us back from our captivity. We are held prisoners with busyness, addictions, social media, and a never-ending list of responsibilities, which pull us further from His presence.

FaithMoves in our prayer closets, in nature, a favorite chair, or anywhere we can go to have intimate time with Him. He yearns for us to come into a deeper relationship. Several passages in the Old Testament say God is a jealous God. Just because we do not have carved statues of wood or stone does not mean we do not worship (even unintentionally) our phones, entertainment, careers, sports, hobbies, and more. Consider the placement of them in your heart and life. Are they distractions? What are our priorities?

Pray

Dear Lord, reveal to me every single thing that keeps me from You. Forgive all the ways I put you in second place or, sadly, even in third. Holy Spirit, convict me in this each day that I will love the Lord God with all my mind, heart, soul, and strength. Thank You, Lord, for always being there when I cry out to you and for the rest and comfort I find in Your presence. In Jesus's name.

Confess

You make me lie down in green pastures;
You lead me beside the still waters. You restore
my soul. (Psalm: 232–3 NKJV)

His Presence will go with me, and He will
give me rest. (Exodus 33:14 NKJV)

17

FaithMoves in Brokenness

Reflect

> The Lord is near to those who have a broken heart and saves such as have a contrite spirit. (Psalm 34:18 NKJV)

> The sacrifices of God are a broken spirit, a broken and a contrite heart—these, O God, You will not despise. (Psalm 51:17 NKJV)

In the moments of genuine brokenness, when we are on our knees crying out to Him in repentance, or deep sorrow, *FaithMoves*. It is right then, when our hearts are broken and open, He draws near to us. Our Father wants to comfort us even if our circumstance cannot be changed, even if we are suffering loss, even if we are experiencing the pain that came from the consequence of our own wrongdoing.

There is a raw quality of brokenness which offers assurance that He alone is our source. Intuitively, we cry out passionately to Him. Our eyes may be swollen from sobbing, and our hope is vanishing as vapor, yet in His presence, we hear Him. We know He is near, and we can trust Him. There is no greater love than this.

Jesus cried out "Abba, Father, all things are possible for You. Take this cup away from Me, nevertheless, not what I will but what

You will" (Mark 14:36 NKJV). Jesus was just as we are in our own despair. In times of sorrow, it can be difficult to regain His perspective. He will help us. The Holy Spirit will comfort us, heal our brokenness, convict us of sin, provide us freedom from strongholds, and anoint us to get up, stand, and move forward in faith.

Pray

Dear Lord, please remind me that You are always with me. When I feel like I just can't do this anymore, when it's just too hard, when I'm frightened, lonely, grieving, or full of remorse, I know that You are with me, and You love me just as I am. I place my broken mess at Your feet, Lord. You are my everything, and I need You every moment of every day. In Jesus's name.

Confess

You, O Lord, are a shield for me, my glory, and the One who lifts up my head. (Psalm 3:3 NKJV)

He will heal my broken heart and bind up my wounds. (Psalm 147:3 NKJV)

18

FaithMoves Speaking
His Word

Reflect

> For the Word of God is living and powerful and sharper than any two-edged sword, piercing even to the division of soul and spirit, and of joints and marrow, and is a discerner of the thoughts and intents of the heart. (Hebrews 4:12 NKJV)

> All Scripture is given by inspiration of God and is profitable for doctrine, for reproof, for correction, for instruction in righteousness that the man of God may be complete, thoroughly equipped for every good work. (2 Timothy 3:16 NKJV)

God created us for His extraordinary purposes. His plans for our lives are more than we can even imagine! He has given us His Word from the beginning of time. He called things into existence. "Then God said…" (Genesis 1 NKJV). His Word is personal just for us, providing His wisdom for every circumstance in life. His Word is the directive and blueprint. His Word is His will. *FaithMoves* in hearing and meditating on the richness of His inspiration. His Word comes alive when we speak it just as He did. Paul teaches in Ephesians 5:17 that the sword of the Spirit is the Word of God. It is our offensive weapon against Satan's tactics. Simple scriptures in our heart can be released when needed. "I bring every thought into captivity to the obedience of Christ" (2 Corinthians 10:5 NKJV).

Our faith deepens as we declare God's Word for our loved ones, for health, for healing, against every negative thought, and for every blessing our heart desires for our family and friends. God's Word was written just for us! His Word is a treasure that we can mine through daily. "For with the heart, one believes unto righteousness, and with the mouth confession is made unto salvation" (Romans 10:10 NKJV). When we speak His Word, we are speaking life into every situation.

————◇◈◇————

Pray

Dear Lord, thank You for Your Word. I know every word is profitable for me because I believe You love me and want me to have blessings and abundance in my life. I believe my *FaithMoves* when I speak Your Word every day. I believe Your Word is the light I need to accomplish the purpose You created me for.

Confess

> When I speak God's Word, it shall not return void but accomplish what He pleases. (Isaiah 55:11 NKJV)

> Your Word is a lamp to my feet and a light to my path. (Psalm 119:105 NKJV)

19

FaithMoves with Courage

Reflect

> Be strong and of good courage, do not fear nor be afraid of them; for the Lord your God, He is the One who goes with you. He will not leave you nor forsake you. (Deuteronomy 31:6 NKJV)

> Fear not, for I am with you; Be not dismayed, for I am your God. I will strengthen you, Yes, I will help you, I will uphold you with My righteous right hand. (Isaiah 41:10 NKJV)

Throughout the Bible, God says, "I am." His promises provide strength, hope, and courage so that we are able to live our lives free from fear. At this writing, fear permeates our world. The COVID-19 pandemic has compromised more than our health. There is an epidemic of fear that has Satan rejoicing. Financial insecurity, fear for our children and families, fear of loss through division, fear of illness, and even death.

In his final exhortation to the Corinthian church, Paul writes, "Watch, stand fast in the faith, be brave, be strong. Let all that you do be done with love" (1 Corinthians 16:13 NKJV), This passage moves us to the present moment like no other. *FaithMoves* in harmony with courage and love. When we stand in this truth, we can be free of fear. We stand with courage. We can resist the devil. His word says perfect love casts out fear.

We live in a culture that wears anxiety as a badge of honor. That is not God's will for us. Jesus said to His apostles, "Let not your heart be troubled, neither let it be afraid" (John 14:27 NKJV). During the storm when the apostles were on the boat and the wind was against them, they saw a figure out on the water and believed it was a ghost. They became frightened not of the storm but of the unknown image. Jesus reassured them, "It is I, do not be afraid" (Matthew 14:27 NKJV).

Pray

Dear Lord, when I am afraid, speak to me and reassure me and give me courage to stand in faith. I know You are always with me, but sometimes when fear overcomes me, I forget. Let Your Words in my heart surface to my mouth and strengthen me. In Jesus's name.

Confess

> I will be of good courage, and God shall strengthen my heart as my hope is in Him. (Psalm 31:24 NKJV)

> Whenever I am afraid, I will trust in You, Lord. (Psalm 56:3 NKJV)

20

FaithMoves in Praise

> O Lord, You are my God. I will exalt You, I will praise Your name. For You have done wonderful things; Your counsels of old are faithfulness and truth. (Isaiah 25:1 NKJV)

> Praise the Lord! Sing to the Lord a new song and His praise in the assembly of saints. For the Lord takes pleasure in His people. (Psalm 149:1,4 NKJV)

The book of Psalms is full of praise and thanksgiving to our Lord God. His power and might throughout creation stir the hearts of His people for Him. Through musical instruments, dance, and song, His name is magnified above the earth. "Then David danced before the Lord with all his might; So David and all the house of Israel brought up the ark of the Lord with shouting and with the sound of the trumpet" (2 Samuel 6: 14–15 NKJV). Nothing pleases God as the sound of our voices are lifted up with focused attention on Him.

FaithMoves as we privately or corporately praise Him. Paul tells us in Hebrews not to forsake the assembling together partly because we need relationship with other believer, but also to come together and sing praises to our Lord. The Holy Spirit arouses us during this time of praise. Satan's tactic is to distract us from praise with a bombardment of thoughts to pull our hearts away from God.

As we enter the presence of God, *FaithMoves* us to a deeper awareness. The still small voice beckons our recognition. We grow in our relationship with Him who knows us. "For You formed my inward parts; You covered me in my mother's womb. I will praise You, for I am fearfully and wonderfully made" (Psalm 139:13–14 NKJV). *FaithMoves* our praise through problems and persecution into God's protection and promises. He is worthy of all praise!

Pray

Dear Lord, I sing praise to you each morning! Thank You for this new day! Forgive me when I am distracted by the things of this world or selfish thoughts that distance us. Draw me close to You and never let me go. In Jesus's name.

Confess

I will praise You, O Lord, with my whole heart; I will tell of all Your marvelous works. (Psalm 9:1 NKJV)

I will bless the Lord, O my soul; And all that is within me, I will bless His holy name! (Psalm 103:1 NKJV)

21

FaithMoves in Worship

Reflect

> But the hour is coming, and now is, when the true worshipers will worship the Father in spirit and truth; for the Father is seeking such to worship Him. God is Spirit, and those who worship Him must worship in spirit and truth. (John 4:23–24 NKJV)

> The secret of the Lord is with those who fear Him, and He will show them His covenant. (Psalm 25:14 NKJV)

In the amplified translation, fear is defined as awe and reverence of our Lord. It is beautiful and sacred to be in His presence and to know the deep things that God reveals to us in worship. When we speak and sing praise to God, it is a one-way attitude to enter in His presence. In worship, our *FaithMoves* us in a communion with Him. Our spirits align with His Spirit. It is often in this place we are able to discern His still small voice.

Before God can transform us, renew us, and restore us, we need to come before Him in repentance with the willingness of a desperate heart. "Behold, You desire truth in the inward parts, and in the hidden part, You will make me know wisdom" (Psalm 51:6 NKJV). This is the way to worship in truth, to get real before Him. Even though He knows anyway, our acknowledgment is what He wants from us.

FaithMoves in the simplicity of worship. To be quiet in your spirit, free from distractions allows rich spiritual dialogue with our Lord. It is during our moments of pure devotion that we find His love alive in us, His joy instilled in us despite our circumstances or our forever changing feelings.

———◇◈◇———

Pray

Dear Lord, I come before you this day with a humble and contrite heart. Thank You for Your truth and Your mercy. Thank You for Your Word. Thank You for Your Holy Spirit. There is no better time spent in my day than my time with You. Forgive me for all the hours I have wasted putting other things before You. In Jesu'ss name.

Confess

> I have grace by which I can serve God acceptably with reverence and godly fear. (Hebrews 12:28 NKJV)

> I worship Him who made heaven and earth, the sea and springs of water. (Revelation 14:7b NKJV)

22

FaithMoves in Miracles

Reflect

> And His name, through faith in His name, has made this man strong, whom you see and know. Yes, the faith which comes through Him has given him this perfect soundness in the presence of you all. (Acts 3:16 NKJV)

> How shall we escape if we neglect so great a salvation, which at first began to be spoken by the Lord, and was confirmed to us by those who heard Him, God also bearing witness both with signs and wonders, with various miracles, and gifts of the Holy Spirit, according to His own will? (Hebrews 2:3–4 NKJV)

After the Holy Spirit appeared to the apostles on the Day of Pentecost in Acts 2, Peter and John healed a lame man in the name of Jesus (Acts 3). As this man had been paralyzed since birth, it was quite a sight for the people to see him running and praising God! Every spiritual gift we receive from the Holy Spirit gives us the ability to manifest miracles in our own lives and in the lives of others, in Jesus's name. *FaithMoves* within us to accomplish what God would have us do.

In the Old Testament, God continually gave signs, wonders, and miracles to His people. In Jesus's ministry, He performed miracle after miracle. It was not meant to cease after the resurrection. The Holy Spirit lives within each of us to continue His work. It is His will for us. Remember, His Word is His will! "For with God, nothing will be impossible" (Luke 1:37 NKJV).

The enemy, Satan, tells us we are not qualified. Jesus said we are: "You shall receive power when the Holy Spirit has come upon you; and you shall be witnesses to Me in Jerusalem, and in all Judea and Samaria, and to the ends of the earth" (Acts 1:8 NKJV). *FaithMoves* with authority in miracles. Allow your life to shine in the power of His will through the spiritual gifts He has given just for you.

Pray

Dear Lord, open my eyes each day to see the miracles all around me. You have a miracle for me with each sunrise, each sunset, each breath I take, and each season I walk with You at my side. Help my faith to grow deeper in understanding of the spirituals gifts You gave me in order to be Your witness today. In Jesus's name.

Confess

God has given me the spirit of wisdom and revelation in the knowledge of Him (Ephesians 1:17 NKJV)

God has done great and awesome things which my eyes have seen. (Deuteronomy 10:21 NKJV)

23

FaithMoves in Sacrifice

> I beseech you, therefore, brethren, by the mercies of God that you present your bodies a living sacrifice, holy, acceptable to God, which is your reasonable service. (Romans 12:1 NKJV)

> Greater love has no one than this than to lay down one's life for his friends. (John 15:14 NKJV)

In the Old Testament, God's people sacrificed through burnt offerings (Leviticus 1:3–17, 6:8–13), grain offerings (Leviticus 2:1–16, 6:14–23), peace offerings (Leviticus 3:1–17, 7:11–34), sin offerings (Leviticus 4:1–35, 6:24–30), and trespass offerings (Leviticus 5:14–6:7, 7:1–7). These offerings were pleasing to Him and spoke prophesy of the coming of Jesus that remain vital considerations for us today. What can we sacrifice for Him? Our time, money, and service? What does it mean to present our bodies as a living sacrifice?

FaithMoves powerfully in sacrifice. To dedicate an hour or more in prayer and worship in His presence will deepen our relationship. Sometimes we fast from food for a meal, a day or several days, or we sacrifice sleep in order to spend time in early morning devotion. Jesus sacrificed His life for our sins. Sacrificing our ordinary fleshly desires with pure intentions is what pleases Him.

Paul writes to the Ephesians to be as children, imitators of God. "Walk in love as Christ also has loved us and given Himself for us, an offering and a sacrifice to God for a sweet-smelling aroma" (Ephesians 5:2 NKJV). Sacrificing our time, using our talents, and financial resources are ways we surrender our selfish desires in service to our family, friends, and others. *FaithMoves* in this sacrifice of wholehearted love.

Pray

Dear Lord, thank You for all You have done for me. Your grace and mercy are new each day. Please remind me to set aside time for You. Remind me to lay aside what I want in order to be there for someone else. I want my life to be a living sacrifice. I want my heart's intentions and motives to be right and not self-seeking. In Jesus's name.

Confess

> I will honor the Lord with my possessions and with the first fruits of all my increase. (Proverbs 3:9 NKJV)

> I will serve you, Lord, for even the Son of Man did not come to be served but to serve and give His life as a ransom for many. (Mark 10:45 NKJV)

24

FaithMoves in Righteousness

Reflect

> No weapon formed against you shall pros-
> per, and every tongue which rises against you
> in judgment, you shall condemn. This is the
> heritage of the servants of the Lord, and their
> righteousness is from Me, says the Lord. (Isaiah
> 54:17 NKJV)

> If we confess our sins, He is faithful and just
> to forgive us our sins and to cleanse us from all
> unrighteousness. (1 John 1:9 NKJV)

When we wholeheartedly accepted Jesus as our Lord and Savior, we
became righteous before God. There is nothing greater than this!
FaithMoves in our salvation. The Holy Spirit will live in us and convict us each and every time we sin or pull away from our relationship
with Him. When we repent, God sees us as righteous in and through
Jesus. This heritage is His promise.

Satan wants to steal our inheritance by polluting our minds
with thoughts of unworthiness, guilt, and condemnation. "The thief
comes to steal and to kill and to destroy" (John 10:10 NKJV). It is
an easy trap to fall into after we sin, make a mistake, or harbor ill will

or judgments against others. Paul encourages us to "be transformed by the renewing of your mind that you may prove what is that good and acceptable and perfect will of God" (Ephesians 12:2b NKJV).

FaithMoves when we ask the Holy Spirit each day to change our hearts, guard our mouths, cleanse our minds, and help us resist Satan. The shield of faith is a powerful weapon of warfare when used with the breastplate of righteousness. We know who we are in Him. As we keep our focus on Jesus, our faith deepens, and we will always be right in His eyes.

Pray

Dear Lord, thank You that I am wonderfully made by You and that I am loved by You. Thank you for the tests and the pruning which are necessary for me to grow closer to You. It is often uncomfortable, yet if it changes me and helps me to be of stronger character. Please don't stop. In Jesus's name.

Confess

A righteous man may fall seven times and rise again. (Proverbs 24:16)

He loves righteousness and justice; the earth is full of the goodness of the Lord. (Psalm 33:5 NKJV)

Aug. 13th 2021

25

FaithMoves in a Breakthrough

Reflect

> Therefore, we also, since we are surrounded by so great a cloud of witnesses, let us lay aside every weight and the sin which so easily ensnares us, and let us run with endurance the race that is set before us. (Hebrews 12:1 NKJV)

> The one who breaks open will come up before them; they will break out, pass through the gate, and go out by it; their king will pass before them with the Lord at their head. (Micah 2:13 NKJV)

———◆◆◆———

A stronghold can be a destructive mindset which Satan uses to control us or render us ineffective for God. Generally, any repetitive sin, addiction, character flaw, gossip, or judgmental attitude that keep us prisoners will sabotage our efforts to be holy. This leads to a vicious cycle of self-condemnation, unworthiness, shame, people-pleasing, self-limitations, depression, and discouragement.

Control
mistrust
anger

Jesus help us! *FaithMoves* like a one-way arrow down a one-way street toward Him. He is the only way. Faith brought us to the cross. The struggle is real. We must open our mouths and call upon His name in our turmoil. Paul emphatically writes to the Corinthians, "For though we walk in the flesh, we do not war according to the flesh. For the weapons of our warfare are not carnal but mighty in God for pulling down strongholds" (2 Corinthians 10:3–4 NKJV).

He is our hope. *FaithMoves* us to a place of desperation where we surrender and allow Him to break down the prison walls as He did for Paul and Silas. Often this requires intense focus through prayer and fasting on our part. Yet when we trust and rely on God, our lives become a testimony to others of victory.

Pray

Dear Lord, I can't do this without you. I have tried over and over, yet I often let You down as I let myself down. Please deliver me and help me break through this stronghold. Lord, I plead Your mercy and grace for this. Break down the walls around my heart. Thank You for this breakthrough. In Jesus's name.

Confess

I will resist the devil, and he will flee from me. (James 4:7 NKJV)

In the day when I cried out, You answered me and made me bold with strength in my soul. (Psalm 138:3 NKJV)

26

FaithMoves in Relationships

Reflect

> Two are better than one because they have a good reward for their labor. For if they fall, one will lift up his companion. But woe to him who is alone when he falls, for he has no one to help him up. Again, if two lie down together, they will keep warm; but how can one be warm alone? Though one may be overpowered by another, two can withstand him. And a threefold cord is not quickly broken. (Ecclesiastes 4:9–12 NKJV)

> If we love one another, God abides in us, and His love has been perfected in us. (1 John 3:12 NKJV)

God's Word instructs us to love. Those people that come in our lives will have varying degrees of significance. Some will be casual and fleeting at specific times. The relationships that God brings to us are integral in developing our character and righteousness in Him. *FaithMoves* in right relationships. When we nourish the soul of another with love, compassion, and connection, this pleases Him.

"It is not good that man should be alone; I will make him a helper comparable to him" (Genesis 2:18 NKJV).

Over and over, it seems that what God created for good and for His pleasure, Satan wants to destroy. Right from the get-go in the garden, jealousy and anger took root in Cain (Genesis 4). Satan is the source of strife, division, judgments, resentments, and selfishness because he seeks to ensnare our minds. As complicated as relationships can be in families, friendships, and marriages, God's will shall triumph in love.

When we seek Him with all our heart, soul, and mind, He will draw us closer to Him and help us. The Holy Spirit will stir our spiritual gifts, and we will develop strength to grow the fruit of the spirit in our relationships. *FaithMoves* to bring Jesus in our bonds with others. In obedience, we forgive. In obedience, we put away childish things. In obedience, we pray. Love matures. Love never fails (1 Corinthians 13:8, 11 NKJV).

Pray

Dear Lord, I want to be Your friend first. I want to be in relationships that draw me closer to You. Please bring the right people in my life that will nourish my soul and help me be a better person. Thank You for these people. May I be a blessing to them. May we help one another, pray together, and make a difference. In Jesus's name.

Confess

I will bear with others, I will forgive others,
I will put on love and let the peace of God rule in
my heart. (Colossians 3:13–15 NKJV)

I will walk in wisdom toward those who
are outside, redeeming the time. (Colossians 4:5
NKJV)

27

FaithMoves in Trust

> Behold, I am with you and will keep you wherever you go and will bring you back to this land; for I will not leave you until I have done what I have spoken to you. (Genesis 28:15 NKJV)

> The Lord is good, a stronghold in the day of trouble; and He knows those who trust in Him. (Nahum 1:7 NKJV)

He promises to never leave us or forsake us. His love for us is unconditional, His purpose and plans for us are for good. Yet do we really trust Him? We want to trust; we say we trust. Yet our will takes over, and we find ourselves managing our own lives once again. Please understand that believing in Jesus and completely surrendering our lives to Him are two different matters. *FaithMoves* with uncertainty through the threshold of the unknown.

God's faithfulness to us is as unconditional as His love. Trust in Him, lean not on your own understanding, acknowledge Him, He will direct your path (adapted from Proverbs 3:5–6). The truth in this verse is renowned because of the revelation and wisdom these words instill in our spirits.

Destroying our trust in God was the first way Satan was successful. Eve doubted God's instruction not to eat from the tree of the knowledge of good and evil. Satan questioned her, "Did God really say that?" (adapted from Genesis 3:1). How often do we hear from God, then quickly dismiss His will, His plan, His ideas for us? *FaithMoves* through trust, enabling us to fulfill the destiny which we were created for.

Pray

Dear Lord, forgive me for all the times I did not trust You, for all the times I took my will back to have things my way. Forgive my impatience when I don't think You are working fast enough. And, Lord, forgive my pride and stubbornness. I am so sorry. Lord, I really need Your help here. Help me to trust You every day beginning today. In Jesus's name.

Confess

I trust in You, O Lord; You are my God. My times are in Your hands. (Psalm 31:14–15 (NKJV)

I trust in Him at all times; I pour out my heart before Him; He is a refuge for me. (Psalm 62:8 NKJV)

28

FaithMoves in Obedience

> Now it shall come to pass, if you diligently obey the voice of the Lord your God, to observe carefully all His commandments which I command you today, that the Lord your God will set you high above all nations of the earth. And all these blessings shall come upon you and overtake you because you obey the voice of the Lord your God. (Deuteronomy 28:1–2 NKJV)

> If anyone loves Me, he will keep My word; and My Father will love him, and We will come to him and make Our home with him. (John 14:23 NKJV)

Obedience is truly an act of faith. Obedience is more than just doing the next right thing, going to church, or volunteering in the community. It encompasses hearing God, then taking action even when it does not make sense, stirs fear, or goes against other people's opinions. *FaithMoves* through obedience to accomplish God's will. Paul writes, "For the gifts and calling of God are irrevocable" (Romans 11:29 NKJV).

God promises us an abundance of blessings for our submission and obedience in every area of our lives. Even when we miss the mark, if our intentions were pure, and our willingness was present, His grace covers us. Obedience is the door into God's heart. Nothing pleases Him more. Jesus's obedience to His Father is our foundation. "This is my beloved Son in whom I am well pleased. Hear Him!" (Matthew 17:5 NKJV)

Rebellion and stubbornness are spirits of the enemy. We can overcome them because the Holy Spirit lives in us. "He who is in you is greater than he who is in the world" (1 John 4:4 NKJV). As we deepen our relationship with Jesus when we come into His presence, these intimacy, stillness, and humility activate the wisdom we need to submit to His promptings. It becomes fluid within us. Living in obedience becomes effortless. Loving, forgiving, giving, praying—*FaithMoves*.

Pray

Dear Lord, please help me be willing and obedient to the irrevocable call on my life. I know that I belong to You, that You love me even when I stumble, even when I defy You. I repent for all times I am rebellious, stubborn, prideful, and disobedient to Your promptings. I ask You now to refine and prune me as only You can. Thank You, Holy Spirit, for conviction, and renew my mind and change my heart. In Jesus's name.

Confess

> I shall keep the commandments of the Lord my God and walk in His ways. (Deuteronomy 8:6 NKJV)

> And this is love that I will walk according to His commandments. (I will walk in love.) (2 John 1:6 NKJV)

29

FaithMoves with Hope

Reflect

> Hope that is seen is not hope; for why does one hope for what he sees? But if we hope for what we do not see, we eagerly wait for it with perseverance. (Romans 8:18 NKJV)

> Now may the God of hope fill you with all joy and peace in believing that you may abound in hope by the power of the Holy Spirit. (Romans 15:13 NKJV)

Our *FaithMoves* Jesus to respond to the hope that dwells in our hearts. Day after day, our prayers and fasting give understanding that He is for us and with us. This in itself is miraculous! Paul writes that we, "being rooted and grounded in love, may be able to comprehend with all the saints what is the width and length and depth and height—to know the love of Christ which passes knowledge that you may be filled with the fullness of God" (Ephesians 3:17b–19 NKJV).

Faith is the candle that burns steadily to provide His light. Hope is the flame. Often Satan attempts to extinguish the flame. Being a thief, he wants to steal our joy, replacing it with a spirit of despair, discouragement, or hopelessness. *FaithMoves* with hope to stand firm in God's promises. Through faith, hope rises above discouragement.

Hope is the morning sunrise in our lives, beckoning a new day. It is anticipation of the loving guidance of His will. Hope stirs us and inspires us to open our hearts. Consider how our faith can instill hope in others, gently lifting up those struggling with encouragement and compassion. "You will show me the path of life; in Your presence is fullness of joy; at Your right hand are pleasures forevermore" (Psalm 16:11 NKJV).

———◇◈◇———

Pray

Dear Lord, You are the lifter of my head. Thank You for the hope I have in Jesus and for all the wonderful days ahead. Your Word encourages me that Your love is everlasting, and I have hope and a future as I call upon You and seek You with all my heart. Thank You, Lord for Your Holy Spirit who continues to show me the way. In Jesus's name.

Confess

I will hold fast to the confession of my hope without wavering, for You are faithful. (Hebrews 10:23 NKJV)

I wait for the Lord, my soul waits, and in His Word I do hope. (Psalm 130:5 NKJV)

30

FaithMoves in Transformation

Reflect

> I will give you a new heart and put a new spirit within you; I will take the heart of stone out of your flesh and give you a heart of flesh. I will put My Spirit within you. (Ezekiel 36:26–27 NKJV)

> But when the kindness and the love of God our Savior toward man appeared, not by works of righteousness which we have done but according to His mercy, He saved us through the washing of regeneration and renewing of the Holy Spirit. (Titus 3:4–5 NKJV)

Because of Jesus, we are miracles. Salvation brought joy and permitted the Holy Spirit entrance to create a clean heart and renew a steadfast spirit within us (Psalm 51:10). Repentance initiated the process to gently prune that which does not bear good fruit. The Holy Spirit convicts us of our wrong-doing and distorted thinking. Acknowledging our sins is the first step necessary for Him to change us.

FaithMoves in His transforming power. We are becoming more and more like Jesus when we surrender to the refiner's fire. What areas of yourself do you seek to eliminate? Where are your weaknesses? By transformation, you leave your past behind and will "be renewed in the spirit of your mind and that you put on the new man which was created according to Go, in true righteousness and holiness" (Ephesians 4:23–24 NKJV).

The Holy Spirit anointed and sent Saul and Barnabas to Cyprus and through the island of Pathos where they met a sorcerer named Elymas. *FaithMoves* through Saul as he called him out for being the son of the devil. It was in that moment Saul was transformed. "Then Saul, who also is called Paul, filled with the Holy Spirit" (Acts 13:9 NKJV). The significance of our obedience expresses desire for a transformation. He loves us so much to mold us for His plans and purpose. "God so loved the world" (John 3:16 NKJV).

Pray

Dear Lord, I surrender to You today that I might be transformed by Your power and Your love. I know this process is often painful, but I desire to live for You and not myself. Help me submit and be in obedience to all You would have me do. Thank You, Holy Spirit, for being my counselor, comfort, and power source. In Jesus's name.

Confess

He knows the way that I take. When He has tested me, I shall come forth as gold. (Job 23:10 NKJV)

I have been crucified with Christ; it is no longer I who live, but Christ lives in me. (Galatians 2:20 NKJV)

31

FaithMoves with Vision

Reflect

> Write the vision and make it plain on tab-
> lets that he may run who reads it. For the vision
> is yet for an appointed time; but at the end, it will
> speak, and it will not lie. Though it tarries, wait
> for it; because it will surely come, it will not tarry.
> (Habakkuk 2:2–3 NKJV)

> Eye has not seen, nor ear heard, nor have
> entered into the heart of man the things which
> God has prepared for those who love Him. But
> God has revealed them to us through His Spirit.
> For the Spirit searches all things, yes, the deep
> things of God. (1 Corinthians 2:9–10 NKJV)

We are only limited by our minds. As we set our thoughts on His Word and His truth, we are thus transformed by the renewal of our minds. *FaithMoves* us to seek His plans and will for our lives. This demands our wholehearted focus. When God created the world, "the earth was without form and void; and darkness was on the face of the deep. And the spirit of God was hovering over the face of the waters" (Genesis 1:2 NKJV). God had a vision for creation!

God knew us before we were born and had a specific purpose for us. It is our job to open our spiritual eyes and see it for ourselves. We have specific abilities, talents, and gifts and will give an account to Him at the end of time as to what we did with them. You must recognize them in yourself first, then believe they will be used to glorify God.

FaithMoves to fulfill our God-given vision when we put Jesus first. The Holy Spirit will propel us with persistence and perseverance whenever Satan attempts to defeat us through fear as the servant in Matthew 25 had done when he buried his talent without cultivating it. Keep your focus on Jesus, and your vision will be covered by His grace.

Pray

Dear Lord, I want to be in the center of Your will. Please forgive me for squandering time and wasting gifts You equipped me to use. Help me see what You see. Help me believe and trust that I can use the abilities and talents in the ways You planned for me. Thank You for this renewed focus and ambition. In Jesus's name.

Confess

> Now faith is the substance of things hoped for, the evidence of things not seen. (Hebrews 11:1 NKJV)

> The Lord makes Himself known to me in a vision; He speaks to me in a dream. (Numbers 12:6 NKJV)

32

FaithMoves in Wholehearted Love

Reflect

> For I am persuaded that neither death nor life, nor angels nor principalities nor powers, nor things present nor things to come, nor height nor depth, nor any other created thing, shall be able to separate us from the love of God which is in Christ Jesus, our Lord. (Romans 8:38 NKJV)

> As the Father loved Me, I also have loved you; abide in My love. If you keep My commandments, you will abide in My love just as I have kept My Father's commandments and abide in His love. (John 15:9 NKJV)

God's Word is a book of His love for His people. "Yes, I have loved you with an everlasting love" (Jeremiah 31:3 NKJV). The rich history from creation to salvation and beyond contained in the Bible declares His glory, majesty, truth, forgiveness, and unconditional love. Why then is it so often that we don't feel His love? This misconception of separation is precisely what Satan wants us to think, planting doubt of God's unconditional agape love and belief that we are unworthy.

FaithMoves us in relationship with Jesus. When we abide in Him, our hearts are open and receptive to the consummation of His love. Paul passionately repeated his appreciation of God's love for us in Ephesians 3:16–19 (NKJV) "that He would grant you, according to the riches of His glory, to be strengthened with might through His Spirit in the inner man, that Christ may dwell in your hearts through faith, that you, being rooted and grounded in love, may be able to comprehend with all the saints what is the width and length and depth and height—to know the love of Christ which passes knowledge, that you may be filled with all the fullness of God."

His love is eternal. He wants to bless us beyond our wildest dreams. Nothing makes Him happier than to see His children prosper and love others the way He loves us. When we bow before Him in devotion or raise our arms in praise, He is exalted, and our love is reciprocal. When we forgive others, obey Him, move in faith and love. His heart rejoices with pleasure and happiness.

Pray

Dear Lord, how I love You and need You every moment of every day. Thank You for always being present in the good times and the bad. Thank You that You never leave me. Even if I push You away, You wait for me. Your everlasting love surrounds me and nourishes my soul. May I also be Your vessel of love to others. In Jesus's name.

Confess

I shall love the Lord my God with all my heart, with all my soul, and with all my mind. (Matthew 22:37 NKJV)

I shall love my neighbor as myself. (Matthew 22:39 NKJV)

33

FaithMoves in His Strength

Reflect

> Likewise the Spirit also helps in our weaknesses. For we do not know what we should pray for as we ought, but the Spirit Himself makes intercession for us with groaning that cannot be uttered. (Romans 8:26 NKJV)

> My grace is sufficient for you, for My strength is made perfect in weakness. Therefore, I take pleasure in infirmities, in reproaches, in needs, in persecutions, in distresses for Christ's sake. For when I am weak, then I am strong. (2 Corinthians 12:9–10 NKJV)

Paul understood that the power of Jesus's resurrection gave him ability to muster strength in all the circumstances he would encounter in his ministry. Like Paul, the knowledge that our life is to be one of service regardless where you are placed, in any season, requires us to be completely dependent on Him. In Romans 7:13–23, Paul laments that the sin that dwells in him often causes him to succumb to his flesh. He knows his reliance must be on Jesus.

Adam and Eve attempted to hide themselves from God behind fig leaves as they knew they were naked. Their flesh failed them which allowed them to doubt God and believe the lies of the serpent. In so many ways, we also hide our own weaknesses with defense mechanisms, ego, materialism, and more. Yet God knows us and meets us in our own overgrown gardens. He gives us the tools necessary for us to rise up and be victorious when we repent and ask for His help.

FaithMoves in the strength of God's sufficiency. His arms hold us, even carry us when we are at our weakest moments. There is no problem too great or heavy for Him to handle. He carried the cross for us. He does not get weary. "He gives power to the weak, and to those who have no might, He increases strength" (Isaiah 31:29 NKJV).

Pray

Dear Lord, thank You for renewing my strength as I wait on You. Thank You for forgiving my weaknesses. How often do I turn to self-reliance and self-sufficiency instead of turning to You? Please forgive me and help me in my weakness. Thank You for the victory that is mine in You. In Jesus's name.

Confess

I can do all things through Christ who strengthens me. (Philippians 4:13 NKJV)

He who is in me is greater than he who is in the world. (1 John 4:4 NKJV)

34

FaithMoves in Humility

> Let nothing be done through selfish ambition or conceit, but in lowliness of mind, let each esteem others better than himself. Let each of you look out not only for his own interests but also for the interests of others. (Philippians 2:3–4 NKJV)

> Be clothed with humility, for God resists the proud but gives grace to the humble. Therefore, humble yourselves under the mighty hand of God that He may exalt you in good time. (1 Peter 5:5b–6 NKJV)

The quality of being humble is a heart condition of altruism. Whereas the qualities of pride and egotism are often selfishness. God has much to say on these. "The fear of the Lord is to hate evil; pride and arrogance and the evil way and the perverse mouth, I hate" (Proverbs 8:13 NKJV). "Pride goes before destruction and a haughty spirit before a fall" (Proverbs 16:18 NKJV).

Satan fell from heaven due to his pride and arrogance. He desired to be exalted above God. This spiritual darkness creates our fleshly self-absorption, self-seeking, self-centered character defects. It may even account for our self-sufficiency instead of trusting and relying on God. *FaithMoves* us into brokenness and a humble heart. "The sacrifices of God are a broken spirit, a broken and a contrite heart—these, O God, You will not despise" (Psalm 51:17 NKJV).

As we pray throughout our day and repent of our selfish attitudes, pride will weaken its hold over us. The Holy Spirit brings new revelation and conviction. Jesus gives us the strength we need to carry the cross of this burden. Sincerely ask Him to show you the ways you are prideful. God promises that when we truly humble ourselves before Him and repent. He will forgive us and hear our prayers.

Pray

Dear Lord, I humble myself before You and ask forgiveness for all the ways pride has been a subtle idol in my life. I don't always recognize it in myself. I prefer to believe I am better than that, but sadly I am not. Please help me with this daily. Do not take the Holy Spirit from me. I need Your grace to help me walk in humility. In Jesus's name.

Confess

I will humble myself in the sight of the Lord, and He will lift me up. (James 4:10 NKJV)

I will do justly, I will be merciful, I will walk humbly with my God. (Micah 6:8b NKJV)

35

FaithMoves in Tribulations

Reflect

> Blessed be the God and Father of our Lord Jesus Christ, the Father of mercies, and God of all comfort, who comforts us in all our tribulation that we may be able to comfort those who are in any trouble with the comfort with which we ourselves are comforted by God. (2 Corinthians 1:3–4 NKJV)

> But may the God of all grace who called us to His eternal glory by Christ Jesus, after you have suffered awhile, perfect, establish, strengthen, and settle you. (1 Peter 5:10 NKJV)

It is through our pain, struggle, and challenges that we tend to seek Him more. In moments of rejection, abandonment, disappointment, and fear, He is with us. Satan seeks to devour us, but God wants us to cast all our cares on Him. Even those we consider the trivial, God cares (1 Peter 5:7). He provides what we need in every situation when we ask Him for help.

We experience His strength and comfort when we go through hard times. We lean on Him, or He carries us. Jesus said, "In the world, you will have tribulation; but be of good cheer, I have overcome the world" (John 16:33 NKJV). Jesus spoke this, and it is truth. *FaithMoves* in the knowledge that our joy cannot be connected to our circumstances.

Without the storms, we would not know calm. Without our trials, we would not experience the moments of comfort that only He can provide. Perhaps He has sent just the right people to console or support us. He knows precisely how to help us. We will then be equipped to use our testimonies to encourage or comfort someone else.

Pray

Dear Lord, so often in the middle of the mess, I allow fear to overcome me. I focus on the problem and not the solution. You are the answer to every question. You are my anchor in every storm. Remind me when I am overcome that You are always alongside of me. You are my ever-present help through every trial and situation. In Jesus's name.

Confess

I will cast my burden on the Lord, and He shall sustain me. (Psalm 55:22 NKJV)

I am hard-pressed but not in despair; persecuted, but not forsaken; struck down, but not destroyed. (2 Corinthians 4:8-9 NKJV)

36

FaithMoves in Our Identity in Jesus

Reflect

> For we are His workmanship created in Christ Jesus for good works, which God prepared beforehand that we should walk in them. (Ephesians 2:10 NKJV)

> Behold what manner of love the Father has bestowed on us that we should be called children of God! Therefore, the world does not know us because it did not know Him. Beloved, now we are children of God; and it has not yet been revealed what we shall be, but we know that when He is revealed, we shall be like Him, for we shall see Him as He is. (1 John 3:1–2 NKJV)

Your identity is more than your job or current role. Those are ever changing in the seasons of life, and often we lose them. The identity we have by faith is eternal. Everything that is right with you is because of who you are in Jesus Christ. Who you are answers every question about why you were born, what your purpose is, and drives us forward. His character is what we strive to become more of.

FaithMoves in our identity in Him. We are nothing less than a miracle. We are called according to His purpose. We are loved and forgiven with His tender mercy. We are reconciled in Him. We are fearfully and wonderfully made! And we have the mind of Jesus as we seek Him with our heart, soul, and strength. The Holy Spirit dwells within us, and as we live for Jesus, we are transformed by this power.

Declare who you really are in Him. Know that you are His beloved and His chosen one. When this truth assimilates into your spirit, the revelation is profound. Seek Him with the passion of a lover. Ask, knock, pray, fast, worship, praise without ceasing. As Paul proclaims, "I press toward the goal for the prize of the upward call of God in Christ Jesus" (Philippians 3:14 NKJV). Indeed, we are His treasures.

Pray

Dear Lord, You are the lover of my soul. I earnestly and humbly surrender to You. Thank You that You created me in Your image and that Your plans for me are good. I pray that my faith deepens each day and pleases You. In Jesus's name.

Confess

I am adopted by Jesus Christ to Himself according to the good pleasure of His will. (Ephesians 1:5b NKJV)

I have been crucified with Christ; it is no longer I who live, but Christ lives in me. I live by faith in the Son of God who loved me and gave Himself for me. (Galatians 2:20 NKJV)

37

FaithMoves in Loss and Grief

Reflect

> For the Lord will not cast off forever. Though He causes grief, yet He will show compassion according to the multitude of His mercies. (Lamentations 3:31–32 NKJV)

> And God will wipe away every tear from their eyes; there shall be no more death, nor sorrow, nor crying. There shall be no more pain, for the former things have passed away. (Revelation 21:4 NKJV)

For the times in life when the unspeakable occur—death of a loved one, loss of health or physical disability, loss of job, career, business, loss through a natural disaster, the list goes on ad infinitum—*FaithMoves* through these days in His compassion and power. Often the season of loss and grief lingers longer than is comfortable. In our brokenness, His love comforts. He sees us. He counts our tears. Perhaps He even cries with us. "Therefore, when Jesus saw her weeping, and the Jews who came with her weeping, He groaned in the spirit and was troubled. Jesus wept, then Jesus, again groaning in Himself, came to the tomb (John 11:33, 35, 38 NKJV).

Jesus teaches His disciples the nature of sorrow becoming joy. Our hearts are designed to feel a spectrum of emotions. "Therefore, you now have sorrow; but I will see you again, and your heart will rejoice, and your joy no one will take from you" (John 16:22 NKJV).

There are hills and valleys in life's wilderness. In Deuteronomy 31:7a–8, Joshua was directed to take God's people into the promised land. "Be strong and of good courage, for you must go with these people to the land which the Lord has sworn to their fathers to give them, and you shall cause them to inherit it. And the Lord, He is the One who goes before you. He will be with you. He will not leave you or forsake you; do not fear or be dismayed." *FaithMoves* in this assurance. Treasure His words in your heart.

Pray

Dear Lord, I know there will always be seasons of transition, loss, and sadness in my life. Thank You for always being there to hold me, Jesus. Thank You for your comfort most, Holy Spirit. You are my source of strength and peace. In Jesus's name.

Confess

> Yea, though I walk through the valley of the shadow of death, I will fear no evil; for You are with me. (Psalm 23:4 NKJV)

> My flesh and my heart fail; But God is the strength of my heart and my portion forever. Psalm 73:26 NKJV)

38

FaithMoves in the Promises of God

Reflect

> Let us hold fast the confession of our hope without wavering, for He who promised is faithful. (Hebrews 10:23 NKJV)

> For all the promises of God in Him are Yes, and in Him, amen to the glory of God through us. (2 Corinthians 1:20 NKJV)

There are over three thousand promises of God in the Bible. That is astounding yet too often overlooked in that, was for then, kind of thinking. What has God promised you? Is there a scripture verse you hold close to your heart? What is prophetic word that was given you? Is His still small voice of knowledge for a specific plan? *FaithMoves* in receiving every promise He gives you without wavering.

Jesus said, "You shall know the truth, and the truth shall make you free. Therefore, if the Son makes you free, you shall be free indeed" (John 8:32, 36 NKJV). Freedom is a promise of God. Just as the Israelites were freed from bondage, we also can be free from our bondages of sin, addictions, pride, anything we are enslaved to.

It is sometimes necessary for us to speak His promises into our lives. "Now the Lord is Spirit; and where the Spirit of the Lord is, there is liberty" (2 Corinthians 3:17 NKJV).

There are multitudes of promises of His protection over us. Confessing Psalm 91 is a powerful prayer for God's protection. "For He shall give His angels charge over you to keep you in all your ways" (Psalm 91:11 NKJV). Scattered throughout His Word are promises to keep us safe, uphold us, strengthen us, help us in times of adversity, and deliver us from the evil one by the blood of Jesus.

Pray

Dear Lord, Your promises overflow like Your love and faithfulness to me. Help me to remember to ask You and then be thankful for all You give to me. Keep my heart humble and always willing to forgive others and repent for my own sins. Release Your divine protection and liberty in those areas I am in bondage. In Jesus's name.

Confess

I will seek You and find You because I search for You with all my heart. (Jeremiah 29:13 NKJV)

The Lord God is a sun and shield; the Lord will give grace and glory; no good thing will He withhold from me if I walk uprightly. (Psalm 84:11 NKJV)

39

FaithMoves in Prayer and Fasting

Reflect

> So He Himself often withdrew into the wilderness and prayed. (Luke 5:16 NKJV)

> Is this not the fast that I have chosen: to loose the bonds of wickedness, to undo the heavy burdens, to let the oppressed go free, and that you break every yoke? (Isaiah 58:6 NKJV)

There is prayer without fasting but not fasting without prayer. During times of fasting, our hearts turn to Him in surrender. When we humbly come before Him in desperation or focused prayer for drawing closer to Him, He will honor our intentions. "For the eyes of the Lord run to and fro throughout the whole earth to show himself strong on behalf of those whose heart is loyal to Him" (2 Chronicles 16:9 NKJV).

FaithMoves in prayer and fasting as we commit to this time with pure motives. We pray and fast for God's direction, vision, answers, or breakthrough for victory over sin or addiction. The Holy Spirit may prompt a fast for intercession in order to pray for a loved one or for spiritual battles or revival. Often, personal repentance and forgiveness are in the forefront before *FaithMoves* in our fast.

There are numerous fasts in the Bible and many resources available to guide you. Fasting is an expectation Jesus has for us. "But you, when you fast, anoint your head and wash your face so that you do not appear to be fasting but to your Father who is in the secret place; and your Father who sees in secret will reward you openly" (Matthew 6:17–18 NKJV). Our heart, commitment to seek Him during prayer and fasting, will bless us with hearing His voice and knowing His will. This two-way communication confirms truth as the Holy Spirit always agrees with God's Word for us.

Pray

Dear Lord, I humble myself before You and repent for everything that keeps us apart. Draw me closer to You during this time. I want to be closer to You. I want to hear Your still small voice. I want to intercede and stand in the gap in Your power for that which You direct my heart to pray. I want this time in prayer and fasting to please You. Please cleanse me, teach me, and reveal to me how You want to use my life. In Jesus's name.

Confess

I will present my body a living sacrifice, holy, acceptable to God. (Romans 12:1 NKJV)

I humble myself with fasting; and my prayer will return to my own heart. (Psalm 35:13 NKJV)

40

FaithMoves in His Peace

Reflect

> Peace I leave with you, My peace I give to you; not as the world gives do I give to you. Let not your heart be troubled, neither let it be afraid. (John 14:27 NKJV)

> You will keep him in perfect peace whose mind is stayed on You because he trusts in You. (Isaiah 26:3 NKJV)

In the middle of the night when you awaken with restless thoughts, His peace is there. When there are struggles in your family or on the job, when finances are tight, during the continual political and social unrest of our times, and anytime Satan attempts to derail us off course of God's direction, we can receive His perfect peace. Paul writes to the Philippians, "Be anxious for nothing but in everything by prayer and supplication with thanksgiving, let your requests be made known to God; and the peace of God, which surpasses all understanding, will guard your hearts and minds through Christ Jesus" (Philippians 4:6–7 NKJV).

Paul writes the antidote to our cares and anxiety, instructing us to meditate on the very things that bring peace to our spirits: truth, nobility, fairness, purity, loveliness, positivity, virtues, and praise. Peace is God's gift to us. Open it, receive it, embrace it.

During times of tribulations, Paul and Silas (prisoners), Daniel (lion's den), David (Goliath), Job (incredible loss), and many others, held the peace of God in their hearts in order to overcome hardships.

There is no such thing as a problem-free life, yet He has given us His strength, the joy of His magnificent creation all around us, and a supernatural peace alive in us from His Spirit. It is all we need. "And He said, My Presence will go with you, and I will give you rest" (Exodus 33:14 NKJV). With thanksgiving, *FaithMoves* in His peace.

Pray

Dear Lord, where would I be without Your love, grace, and peace? With reverence and awe, I come into Your presence; with gratitude, I accept Your good and perfect gifts. My heart overflows in love as my friendship with You matures and as my faith in who You are deepens. Thank You, Father God. Thank You, Jesus. Thank You, Holy Spirit.

Confess

The God of peace Himself will sanctify me completely. (1 Thessalonians 5:33 NKJV)

Quietness and confidence shall be my strength. (Isaiah 30:15 NKJV)

Faith believes the unseen. Faith
hears the unheard.
                                —Jentezen Franklin

Don't doubt in the dark what God
has told you in the light.
                                —Kirk Winters

Faith moves each day you make the
decision to seek Him first.
                                —Teri Gallo Blackadar

With love and gratitude,
Teri

ABOUT THE AUTHOR

Teri Gallo Blackadar has a passion for Jesus, faith, family, and friends. Her nursing career provided deep insights into the various stages and seasons of life. She is an author of assorted essays on nursing, beloved dogs, addiction, and recovery. Teri's heart belongs to Maine where she lives with her yellow Lab, Joe.

CPSIA information can be obtained
at www.ICGtesting.com
Printed in the USA
JSHW010909120421
13405JS00005B/47